# Homemade Ice Cream Cookbook

*Top 50 Ice Cream Recipes*

*for Healthy Families*

**Patrice Clark**

## Your Gift!

We want to show our appreciation that you support our work, so we have put together a gift for you.

Just visit the link on the last page of this book to download it now.

We know you will love this gift.

Thanks!

# Table of Content

## ABOUT — 6

Chocolate-Orange Ice Cream — 7

Dietary Banana Ice Cream — 9

Green Tea Ice Cream — 11

Homemade Vanilla Ice Cream with Chocolate Sauce — 13

Fruit Ice Cream — 16

Basil Ice Cream — 18

Classic Homemade Ice Cream — 20

Stracciatella Ice Cream — 22

Yogurt Ice Cream with Avocado and Cucumber — 24

Lavender Ice Cream — 26

Frozen Yogurt Dessert in Orange Halves — 28

Frozen Yogurt with Egg Whites — 29

Frozen Yogurt with Vanilla — 31

Delicious Homemade Frozen Yogurt with Dried Fruits and Almonds — 33

Frozen Yogurt with Orange, Almonds and Melissa — 35

Frozen Yogurt with Cocoa — 36

Frozen Yogurt with Mango — 38

Beet Frozen Yogurt — 39

| | |
|---|---|
| **Frozen Yogurt with Kiwi** | 41 |
| **Frozen Yogurt with Strawberry** | 42 |
| **Lemon Gelato** | 44 |
| **Pistachio Gelato** | 45 |
| **Cherry Gelato** | 47 |
| **Chocolate Gelato** | 49 |
| **Sea Buckthorn Gelato** | 51 |
| **Saffron Gelato** | 53 |
| **Black Gelato** | 55 |
| **Carrot Gelato** | 57 |
| **Banana-Cinnamon Gelato** | 59 |
| **Delicate Gelato with Pineapple and Coconut Milk** | 61 |
| **Blackcurrant Sorbet with Red Wine** | 63 |
| **Orange-Honey Sorbet** | 64 |
| **Redcurrant Sorbet** | 66 |
| **Mango-Peach Sorbet** | 67 |
| **Watermelon Sorbet with Mint** | 68 |
| **Sparkling Wine Sorbet** | 70 |
| **Strawberry Sorbet** | 71 |
| **Raspberry Sorbet** | 73 |
| **Melon Sorbet** | 74 |
| **Blueberry Sorbet** | 76 |

| | |
|---|---:|
| Granite Carcade | 77 |
| Granite with Lime and Orange | 79 |
| Peach Granita | 80 |
| Coffee Granite | 82 |
| Pomegranate Granita | 83 |
| Apple Granita | 85 |
| Granita with Spicy Wine | 87 |
| White Grape Granita | 88 |
| Watermelon Granita | 90 |
| Grapefruit Granita | 91 |

## DEDICATION

We dedicate this book to our family,
our parents and children.

# About

Patrice and her husband, Andrew are a beautiful and happy American family.

They have two children and Labrador dog. They Live together, Eat together, Pray together, Love together!

When Patrice was a child, she liked to cook different dishes, of course with her mother's help.

When she became a teenager, she decided to devote her life to cooking. Last 15 years she was cooking at her own restaurant.

Andrew meet Patrice in the kitchen at the school of culinary skills in Paris. City of love, romanticism, and French cuisine. It became a fatal meeting.

All recipes written by Patrice and Andrew are straightforward and with an unusual taste.

Everything is brought together in them: love, the energy of creativity, and cumulative 35 years of experience in culinary art.

Enjoy the Recipes of Patrice & Andrew!

# Chocolate-Orange Ice Cream

*Prep Time:* 15 minutes

*Total Time:* 10 hours 15 minutes

*Serves: 2*

*Effort: Not much*

**Ingredients:**
- 1 avocado, peeled and pitted, cut in chunks
- 3 tablespoons cocoa
- 1 orange juice
- 1 orange zest
- ¼ cup bittersweet chocolate
- 3 tablespoons honey

**Directions:**
1. Combine avocado, cocoa, orange zest, juice and honey in a blender and puree until smooth.
2. Chop the chocolate, add it to the mixture, stir thoroughly and put into a freezer for 6-10 hours.
3. Mix your ice cream every hour or place it into an ice cream maker and freeze according to manufacturer's directions

Note: Chocolate should contain at least 70% cocoa. Ideally organic. Avocado should be ripe, otherwise, the ice cream will be spoiled. Instead of honey, you can use syrup Sorgo, syrup Agave. Before freezing it is necessary to try and make sure that sweets and all the tastes you want are enough.

# Dietary Banana Ice Cream

*Prep Time:* 5 minutes

*Total Time: about 2 hours*

*Serves: 2*

*Effort: Not much*

**Ingredients:**
- 2 big bananas
- a pinch of ground cinnamon
- ½ cup natural yogurt
- sugar substitute to taste

**Directions:**
1. Cut two ripe bananas into small pieces and put in a freezer for several hours.
2. Get the frozen banans pieces of bananas out of the freezer, place in a blender along with cinnamon and yogurt or fermented baked milk. Other ingredients - to taste: cognac, peanut butter, vanilla extract, nuts.
3. Whisk the mixture. You need to calculate the amount of liquid components so that its consistency looks like a slightly melted ice cream.

# Green Tea Ice Cream

*Prep Time:  15 minutes*

*Total Time: about 3 hours*

*Serves: 4*

*Effort: Not much*

**Ingredients:**
- 1 quart whole milk
- 5 teaspoons green tea
- 7 tablespoons sugar
- ½ condensed milk

**Directions:**
1. Warm the milk not allowing a boil. Put the tea and sugar into hot milk. Cover and let steep for 30 minutes.
2. Strain the milk, add condensed milk, pour into a container and freeze.
3. Once the mixture is solidified, unfrozen it slightly and put into a blender. Beat on a high speed until a creamy mass is formed.
4. Pour the ice cream into molds and leave in the freezer for 2 hours more.

# Homemade Vanilla Ice Cream with Chocolate Sauce

***Prep Time:*** *30 minutes*

***Serves:*** *4*

***Effort:*** *Not much*

**Ingredients:**
### *For ice cream:*
- 1 and 1/2 cup whole milk
- 1 cup heavy cream
- 1 pod vanilla
- 4 egg yolks
- ½ cup sugar
- whipped cream to garnish

- chopped nuts to garnish
- chocolate chips to garnish

*For sauce:*

- ¼ cup heavy cream
- 2/3 cup whole milk
- 9 ounces dark chocolate, chopped
- 1 tablespoon brandy or rum

**Directions:**

1. In a medium saucepan, mix a cup milk and heavy cream. Cut vanilla pod in halves, scrape seeds and add everything to the milk mixture. Warm until foam forms around the edges but don't bring to a boil. Remove from heat and set aside to steep for 10 minutes.
2. Meanwhile in a bowl, beat the egg yolks and sugar until frothy. Gradually pour the warm milk into the egg yolks, whisking constantly.
3. Return mixture back to the saucepan; cook over medium heat, stirring constantly for 5-7 minutes until it coats the back of the spoon.
4. Remove from the heat. Strain through a sieve into a glass bowl placed in an ice bath.

5. Cover and chill for several hours.
6. Pour the mixture into an ice cream maker, and freeze according to the manufacturer's instructions.
7. Cook a chocolate sauce for homemade ice cream. Mix milk and cream in a saucepan, bring to a boil and immediately remove from heat. Add the chocolate and alcohol stir until smooth.
8. Chill glasses, fill each glass with 4 teaspoons of chocolate sauce, top with 2 balls of ice cream and pour with chocolate sauce.
9. Garnish with whipped cream, nuts and chocolate chips.

# Fruit Ice Cream

*Prep Time: 15 minutes*

*Total Time: 12 hours 15 minutes*

*Serves: 2*

*Effort: Some*

**Ingredients:**
- ½ apple
- 2 bananas
- ½ orange
- 2 tablespoons lemon zest
- 2 tablespoons Sorghum syrup
- 1 tablespoon lemon juice

**Directions:**
1. Peel bananas and cut them into big chunks, place into a container and drizzle with lemon juice to prevent darkening.
2. Peel orange and apple, thoroughly getting rid of all inner rinds, seeds and core. Cut them into chunks and add to the bananas in the container.
3. Cover the container and freeze the fruits for several hours or overnight.
4. Before removing the fruits out of freezer, prepare a syrup. Combine Sorghum syrup with lemon juice.
5. Grind the frozen fruits in a food processor, stopping to scrape down sides.
6. Stir in the syrup and process the mixture for 1-2 minutes more.
7. Transfer the mixture to the freezer for a couple of hours.
8. Take it out and puree in a blender until smooth( approximately 3 minutes)
9. Scoop the ice cream and garnish with sprig of mint, some nuts and fruits.

# Basil Ice Cream

*Prep Time: 1 hour 30 minutes*

*Serves: 12*

*Effort: Not much*

**Ingredients:**
- 3/4 cup sugar
- 1 quart whole milk
- 1 cup basil
- 14 egg yolks

**Directions:**
1. Combine 1/4 cup sugar and milk. Constantly stirring, bring it to a boil, then add finely chopped basil (leave one sprig to garnish) to the

mixture. Remove from heat, cover and let steep for 10 minutes.
2. Separate the egg whites from the yolks. Mix the yolks with the remaining sugar. Once again bring the milk to a boil, pour it into the egg-sugar mixture.
3. Warm the mixture up to 183°F using a water bath.
4. Line your mesh strainer with a double-layer of cheesecloth and strain the mixture after removing it from the water bath.
5. Place to refrigerator to chill overnight.
6. Pour the mixture into the bowl of an ice cream maker and spin according to the manufacturer's instructions.
7. Scoop your ice cream and garnish with a sprig of basil.

# Classic Homemade Ice Cream

*Prep Time: 2 hours 30 minutes*

*Total Time:*

*Serves: 6*

*Effort: Not much*

**Ingredients:**
- 1 and ¼ cups heavy cream
- 2/3 cup sugar
- 1 teaspoon vanilla
- 3 egg yolks
- ½ cup whole milk

**Directions:**
1. Boil the milk. Let it cool.

2. Combine milk with 3 egg yolks, sugar and some vanilla.
3. Place the mixture on a water bath and constantly stirring cook it until the consistency of evaporated milk.
4. Whisk the cream but don't allow it to become butter.
5. Combine two mixtures and accurately stir them. Transfer to your freezer for an hour.
6. In an hour scrape it into the bowl of your ice cream maker and churn according to the manufacturer's instructions.
7. Scoop the ice cream and serve. Garnish with any fruits or nuts, or flowers if desired.

# Stracciatella Ice Cream

***Prep Time: 6 hours***

***Serves: 4***

***Effort: Not much***

**Ingredients:**
- 7/8 cup whole milk
- 1 and ½ cup heavy cream
- 4 egg yolks
- ¾ cup sugar
- 2 ounces good quality dark chocolate, finely chopped

**Directions:**
1. Mix milk and cream In a saucepan. Bring to a boil over medium-high heat.

2. Whisk yolks and sugar in a big bowl. Beat until the mixture has pale yellow creamy consistency.
3. Once the milk mixture starts to boil, remove it from the heat. Gradually pour hot milk mixture into the egg yolks, constantly stirring. (While stirring, hold the whisk vertically, otherwise, bubbles will form on the surface of the future ice cream).
4. Pour the mixture back into the saucepan. Cook over the medium heat, constantly stirring with a wooden spoon, not allowing a boil. Once the mixture has thickened and coats the spoon the cream is ready.
5. Chill the cream using an ice bath. For this purpose fill a large bowl with very cold water and ice to the half. Place the saucepan with your cream on the top of it. Stir the cream from time to time for 30-40 minutes until it cools. Stirring will prevent the crystallization of the ice cream.

6. Remove the pan with ice cream from a water bath, cover tightly and place into a refrigerator to chill for 4-5 hours more.
7. After that churn it according to manufacturer's instructions for 20 to 40 minutes. In the end of churning process add chocolate chips.
8. Transfer to a freezer safe container, drizzling a bit of remaining chocolate on top, and freeze 3 to 4 hours or overnight until firm.

## Yogurt Ice Cream with Avocado and Cucumber

*Prep Time:* 25 minutes

*Total Time: about 12 hours*

*Serves: 2*

*Effort: Not much*

**Ingredients:**
- 1 ripe avocado
- 1/3 cup sugar
- 1 tablespoon vanilla sugar
- 1 large size cucumber
- 6 tablespoons lime juice
- 2/3 cup dessert yogurt

**Directions:**
1. Peel avocado. Remove the pit, chop the pulp into small cubes.
2. Peel the cucumber and remove the seeds with teaspoon if necessary. Chop in small cubes as well.
3. Combine avocado and cucumber in the bowl of a food processor
4. Add lime juice and process until smooth.
5. Stir plain and vanilla sugar into the mixture, churn again, then add yogurt and process until frothy.

6. Transfer the mixture to a sealed container and place to a freezer for nine hours. Every 3 hours, stir it thoroughly with a fork or whisk with a blender to get rid of the ice crystals.
7. Half an hour before serving remove the mixture from freezer to refrigerator. Allow it to defrost slightly before scooping.
8. Scoop your ice cream and garnish with sprig of fresh mint.

## Lavender Ice Cream

*Prep Time: 1 hour 30 minutes*
*Total Time: 5-8 hours*
*Serves: 12*

*Effort: Not much*

**Ingredients:**
- 2/3 cup honey
- 1 and 1/3 cup sugar
- 1 and 2/3 cup milk
- 14 egg yolks
- 1 teaspoon baking powder
- 1 tablespoon dried lavender flowers
- 1 teaspoon soda
- 1 and 1/3 cup heavy cream

**Directions:**
1. Make caramel with honey and lavender: warm until honey starts to bubble and thicken. Pour in milk and cream, bring to a boil, remove from heat and set aside to steep for 20 minutes.
2. Strain the mixture, bring to boil again and add yolks. Constantly stirring, warm the mixture on a water bath up to 183°F, then strain it again and let to cool on an ice bath in the refrigerator overnight.
3. The next day churn it in your ice cream maker according to the manufacturer's directions.
4. Scoop and garnish with a sprig of lavender.

# Frozen Yogurt Dessert in Orange Halves

*Prep Time: 30 minutes*

*Total Time: 5-8 hours*

*Serves: 6*

*Effort: Not much*

**Ingredients:**
- 3 cups nonfat plain yogurt
- 3 oranges
- 1/4 cup sugar
- 1 teaspoon vanilla extract
- chocolate chips to garnish if desired

**Directions:**

1. Accurately cut the orangs in two halves and take the flesh out. Place skin halves into the refrigerator and squeeze juice out of pulp.
2. Combine yogurt, orange juice, sugar and vanilla extract in a large bowl and stir it thoroughly until sugar dissolves.
3. Transfer the mixture into an airtight container and place to freezer for 5-8 hours to firm.
4. Scoop and serve.
5. You may garnish your dessert with chocolate chips, nuts etc. Or just enjoy its pure delicious taste. Bon Appetite!

## Frozen Yogurt with Egg Whites

*Prep Time: 30 minutes*

*Serves: 12*

*Effort: Not much*

**Ingredients:**
- 2/3 cup sugar
- 2 egg whites
- 2½ cups yogurt
- ¼ cup water

**Directions:**
1. Cook syrup with water and sugar. After sugar completely dissolves , steam 1 minute more.
2. Whisk the whites until thick frothy.
3. Keep whisking and gradually pour the syrup in. Whisk until the mixture cools completely.
4. Stir in the yogurt.
5. Transfer the chilled mixture to an ice-cream maker, and freeze according to the manufacturer's directions.
6. Serve with fruits, chocolate or jam.

# Frozen Yogurt with Vanilla

*Prep Time: 28 hours*

*Total Time: 28 hours*

*Serves: 8*

*Effort: medium*

**Ingredients:**
- 1 quart whole milk
- 1 and ¼ plain natural yogurt
- ½ cup sugar
- 1 vanilla pod
- 3 tbsp. L. Maple syrup or liquid honey
- confectionery crumbles for garnish

**Directions:**
1. Warm milk up to 180°F, then cool it to 100-110°F.
2. Stir in natural yogurt into the warm milk and mix thoroughly.
3. Pour the mixture into jars and place to the yogurt maker for 8-12 hours.
4. Once the yogurt is ready, line your mesh strainer with a double-layer of cheesecloth, spoon the yogurt in and let it sit propped over a bowl in the refrigerator overnight until all water has drained out.
5. The next morning process ½ cup sugar with vanilla pod a food processor until smooth. Stir in this aromatic flour into the yogurt, add 3 tablespoons L.
6. Maple syrup or liquid honey and whisk thoroughly in a food processor or blender.
7. Pour the mixture into an ice-cream maker, and freeze according to the manufacturer's directions.
8. Scoop frozen yogurt, garnish with confectionery crumbles and serve.

# Delicious Homemade Frozen Yogurt with Dried Fruits and Almonds

***Prep Time:* 2 hours 30 minutes**

***Total Time:* 5-6 hours**

***Serves:* 5**

***Effort:* Easy**

**Ingredients:**
- 3 ½ cups natural yogurt
- ¼ cup any syrup or liquid honey
- ¼ cup white sugar
- 1 teaspoon vanilla extract
- zest from 1 lemon

- 2 tablespoon lemon juice
- dried fruits and nuts for garnish

**Directions:**
1. Line your strainer with a double-layer of cheesecloth, spoon the yogurt on it and let it sit propped over a bowl in the refrigerator until extra water has drained out for an hour or two.
2. Replace your yogurt into a bowl and whisk for 2-3 minutes until frothy.
3. Stir in sugar, syrup, vanilla extract, lemon juice and zest, and whisk for several minutes more.
4. Pour the mixture into an ice-cream maker, and freeze according to the manufacturer's directions.
5. Serve your dessert immediately or transfer into airtight container and place into freezer to firm completely.
6. Garnish with any dried fruits or/and nuts while serving.

# Frozen Yogurt with Orange, Almonds and Melissa

*Prep Time:* 20 minutes

*Total Time: 5-8 hours*

*Serves: 6*

*Effort: Not much*

**Ingredients:**
- 4 cups yogurt
- 1 and 1/3 cups evaporated sweeten milk
- 2 oranges
- ½ cup toasted almonds
- Melissa for garnish

**Directions:**

1. Combine chopped almonds with yogurt
2. Take zest from oranges, squeeze out juice.
3. Whisk evaporated milk with orange zest and juice.
4. Stir in the mixture yogurt with almonds. Churn it thoroughly.
5. Pour the mixture into an airtight container and leave it in the freezer overnight. Evaporated milk allows the yogurt to freeze evenly, without additional stirring in the process.
6. Scoop once your yogurt is ready, garnish with a sprig of Melissa and serve.

## Frozen Yogurt with Cocoa

**Prep Time:** 30 minutes

**Total Time:**

**Serves: 8**

**Effort: Not much**

**Ingredients:**

- 1 and 1/3 cup yogurt
- ½ cup good dark chocolate
- ½ cup sour cream
- ½ teaspoon vanilla
- 2 tablespoon cocoa powder
- a pinch of sault

**Directions:**
1. Melt the chocolate on water bath and pour it into the sour cream.
2. Combine cocoa powder with a pinch of sault and stir in the mixture.
3. Add yogurt and vanilla. Whisk everything in a food processor.
4. Cover and let sit in a fridge for an hour.
5. Whisk again and place into freezer for 4-5 hours.
6. Scoop and garnish with chocolate chips.

# Frozen Yogurt with Mango

***Prep Time:* 20 minutes**

***Total Time:***

***Serves: 5***

***Effort: Not much***

**Ingredients:**

- 3 mango
- ½ cup cane sugar
- 1 and 1/3 cups natural yogurt
- 1 teaspoon lemon juice

**Directions:**

1. Peel the mangos and chop it in small cubes.

2. Combine with cane sugar and stir in a bowl until sugar dissolves completely.
3. Set aside for two hours. Stir from time to time.
4. Place the fruit mixture into the food processor. Add yogurt, lemon juice and puree until smooth and creamy.
5. Freeze for 4-5 hours.

## Beet Frozen Yogurt

*Prep Time: 1 hour 30 minutes*
*Total Time: 4-5 hours*
*Serves: 4*
*Effort: Some*
**Ingredients:**

- 2 large beets
- 1 and ½ cups natural yogurt
- ¼ cup cane sugar

**Directions:**
1. Preheat oven to 400 °F.
2. Roast your beets in an aluminum foil for 40-50 minutes until soft.
3. Let chill for half an hour and peel them.
4. Place the beets into your food processor and puree for 3-5 minutes until smooth.
5. Let the mixture cool completely.
6. Stir in the yogurt and sugar and puree for some minutes more.
7. Pour the mixture into your ice cream maker and spin according to the manufacturer's instructions.
8. Serve immediately or freeze to serve later.

# Frozen Yogurt with Kiwi

*Prep Time: 15 minutes*

*Total Time:*

*Serves: 10*

*Effort: Not much*

**Ingredients:**
- 8 Kiwifruits
- 1 and ½ cups natural yogurt
- 1 and ½ heavy cream
- 1 cup sugar
- mint for garnish

**Directions:**

1. Peel Kiwifruits and chop them in small cubes or just mash with a fork.
2. Combine fruits, cream, yogurt and sugar in a food processor and puree until smooth and creamy.
3. Pour the mixture into the bowl of an ice cream maker and spin according to the manufacturer's instructions until yogurt is chilled.
4. Serve immediately or transfer to the freezer to harden.
5. Garnish with a sprig of mint.

## Frozen Yogurt with Strawberry

**Prep Time:** 20 minutes

**Total Time:**

**Serves: 4**

**Effort: Not much**

**Ingredients:**
- 1 cup natural yogurt
- 1 cup heavy cream
- 1 cup strawberries
- 2/3 sugar powder

**Directions:**
1. Puree strawberries in a food processor uuntil smooth.
2. Stir in sugar powder, yogurt and cream. Keep stirring .
3. Pour the mixture into airtight container and place to a freezer for 2 hours.
4. Whisk your mixture thoroughly and return to the freezer for a couple of hours again.
5. Do it several times.
6. Before serving garnish with raw strawberry and mint.

# Lemon Gelato

**Prep Time: 3 hours**
**Total Time:**
**Serves: 8**
**Effort: Some**
**Ingredients:**
- 4 lemons
- 1 quart heavy cream
- 10 egg yolks
- 10 egg whites
- ¾ cup powdered sugar
- ¾ cup vanilla sugar
- chocolate chips for garnish

**Directions:**
1. Zest lemons and squeeze out the juice.
2. Combine zest and juice and set aside.
3. Whisk cream with powdered sugar.
4. Whisk whites with sugar until frothy.
5. Slightly whisk yolks with a pinch of sugar.
6. Add whipped yolks and whites to the cream and gradually churn.
7. Stir in lemon zest and juice and keep churning.
8. Place the mixture to the freezer for 3-4 hours or overnight.
9. Scoop, garnish with chocolate chips and serve.

# Pistachio Gelato

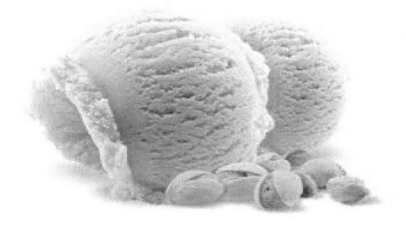

***Prep Time:** 4 hours*
***Total Time:** 5-8 hours*
***Serves:** 4*
***Effort:** Not much*
***Ingredients:***
- 2 cups pistachios
- ½ cup sugar
- 3 cups milk
- a pinch of sault
- 1 tablespoon corn starch
- 1 tablespoon lemon juice

**Directions:**
1. In a saucepan, bring water to a boil. Put the pistachios in and cook for 2-3 minutes.
2. Rinse under cold water in a colander. Peel and dry properly.
3. Place pistachios, ¼ cup sugar and a pinch of salt into the bowl of your food processor, process until finely crushed and the mixture is paste-like.
4. Dissolve the starch in a small amount of milk. Stir properly and set aside.

5. The rest of milk heat in a saucepan over medium-low heat. Add sugar to the warm milk. Bring to a boil and stir in the dissolved starch Cook for 3 minutes stirring constantly until thick enough to coat the back of a spoon.
6. Combine mixture with the pistachio paste, stir and add lemon juice.
7. Pour into the bowl of an ice cream maker and churn according to the manufacturer's instructions.
8. The use of milk instead of cream makes Gelato less fat, but not less tasty! Bon Appetite.

## Cherry Gelato

*Prep Time:* 30 minutes

*Total Time: about 5 hours*

*Serves: 2*

*Effort: Not much*

**Ingredients:**
- 2 ½ cups whole milk
- 5 egg yolks
- 1 cup white sugar
- 2 cups cherries, pitted and halved
- juice out of ½ lemon
- 1 tablespoon rum if desired
- chocolate and whole cherries for garnish

**Directions:**
1. Bring milk to a boil. Set aside.
2. Whisk eggs with ½ cup sugar until frothy.
3. Gradually pour milk into the whipped eggs, constantly stirring.
4. Put on heat and cook until thicken. Keep stirring with a wooden spoon.
5. Chill the mixture.
6. Place cherries into a saucepan. Add lemon juice and the rest of sugar. Bring to a boil. Cook over a medium heat for 10-15 minutes. Chill.

7. Puree cherries along with syrup in a blender.
8. Combine milk mixture, cherries and rum (if desired) and stir thoroughly.
9. Transfer airtight container with your gelato into a freezer and stir it every 30 minutes or pour into the bowl of an ice cream maker and churn according to the manufacturer's instructions. Garnish with melted chocolate and whole cherries.

## Chocolate Gelato

*Prep Time: 15 minutes*
*Serves: 4*
*Effort: Not much*

**Ingredients:**
- 2/3 cup dark chocolate
- ½ cup cocoa powder
- 2 cups milk
- ¾ cup sugar
- a pinch of salt
- 4 egg yolks

**Directions:**
1. Whisk 1 cup milk with cocoa powder and a pinch of salt in a saucepan.
2. Bring to a boil and pour into the bowl with finely chopped chocolate. Stir until smooth.
3. In the same saucepan heat 1 cup milk with sugar until sugar completely dissolves.
4. Whisk egg yolks and slowly pour into the milk mixture, constantly stirring.
5. Return the egg-milk mixture to the saucepan and cook over medium-low heat constantly stirring with a wooden spoon until thick and coats the back of the spoon.
6. Pour the custard into the chocolate mixture through a sieve

7. Churn thoroughly and chill over the ice bath.
8. Cover and place into a freezer till completely firm or use your ice maker and follow the manufacturer's instructions.
9. Keep prepared gelato in an airtight container in the freezer. Defrost a little bit before serving.

## Sea Buckthorn Gelato

*Prep Time: 1 hour 20 minutes*
*Total Time: 3-5 hours*
*Serves: 10*
*Effort: Not much*
**Ingredients:**
- 2 cups sea buckthorns

- 1 cup whole milk
- 1 cup heavy cream
- 5 egg yolks
- ¼ cup sugar
- 2 tablespoons honey

**Directions:**
1. Puree sea buckthorn in a blender and pour through a fine strainer.
2. Combine milk, sugar and ½ cup cream in a saucepan, bring almost to a boil and remove from heat.
3. Whisk egg yolks in a separate bowl and gradually pour the hot milk mixture into the bowl. Stir constantly with a whisk.
4. Now pour the egg-milk mixture back to the saucepan and simmer, constantly stirring until thick enough to coat the back of a spoon.
5. Pour the custard into remaining cream through a sieve. Add honey, sea buckthorn puree and stir.
6. Transfer the mixture into the bowl of the ice cream maker and freeze according to the manufacturer's instructions.
7. Serve, garnished with honey if you like.

# Saffron Gelato

*Prep Time:* **2 hours**

*Total Time:* **5-8 hours**

*Serves:* **10**

*Effort:* **Not much**

**Ingredients:**
- 1 cup milk
- 2 ½ cups heavy cream
- 2/3 cup sugar
- 1 teaspoon natural saffron threads
- 5 egg yolks
- ½ cup pine nuts

**Directions:**
1. Bring milk, sugar and half of cream almost to a boil over medium-low heat.
2. Pound saffron in a mortar and add to the hot milk mixture. Cover and set aside to steep.
3. Once more bring the mixture almost to a boil.
4. Whisk eggs yolks in a bowl. Constantly stirring pour the hot milk mixture into egg yolks.
8. Return the mixture to the saucepan and simmer it until thick enough to coat the back of a spoon. Keep stirring all the time.
5. Once the custard is ready pour it through a fine sieve into the remaining cream.
6. Pour the mixture into the ice maker and churn according to the manufacturer's instructions.
7. Once your ice maker says it's time to add ingredients, stir in the toasted pine nuts.

# Black Gelato

*Prep Time: 45 minutes*

*Total Time: 3-5 hours*

*Serves: 4*

*Effort: Not much*

**Ingredients:**
- 2/3 cup poppy seeds
- 7/8 cup cane sugar
- 1 tablespoon vanilla sugar
- 1/3 powdered sugar
- 2-3 drops rum flavor extract
- 1 1/3 cup heavy cream
- 1 teaspoon cream thickener

- dark chocolate and fresh mint for garnish

**Directions:**

1. Pour poppy seeds with boiling water and set aside until the moisture is absorbed, and the seeds swell.
2. Beat poppy seeds in a blender with cane and vanilla sugars.
3. Chill the heavy cream in a fridge, than beat them in the blender with powdered sugar, cream thickener and rum flavor extract.
4. Churn milk and poppy mixtures and transfer into an airtight container and leave in a freezer until completely firm or place it into your ice cream maker, choose the button "Gelato" and freeze it according to the manufacturer's instructions.
5. Black gelato is ready! Scoop and serve garnished with dark chocolate and a sprig of fresh mint. Bon Appetite!

# Carrot Gelato

*Prep Time:* 1 hour 35 minutes

*Total Time: 5-8 hours*

*Serves: 10*

*Effort: Not much*

**Ingredients:**
- 1 pound carrot
- 6 egg yolks
- ½ cup sugar
- 1 and 1/3 cream
- 1 cup milk
- 1 tablespoon orange zest
- one cinnamon stick

- 1 teaspoon vanilla

**Directions:**
1. Peel the carrot. Chop it in small cubes. Place into a saucepan, add ¼ cup water, cover and simmer until it is completely soft.
2. Heat milk in a small saucepan, add cinnamon, orange zest and set aside to steep for 30 minutes.
3. Place the carrot into a blender bowl, add cream and beat until completely smooth.
4. Pour the milk through a sieve to remove zest and cinnamon and heat it up to boil.
5. Whisk egg yolks in a bowl. Constantly stirring pour hot milk into the egg yolks.
6. Return the mixture to the pan and stirring, cook over medium heat until thickens and coats the back of a spoon.
7. Ready custard pour into cream-carrot mixture through a sieve, mix thoroughly.
8. Place to your ice maker and churn according the manufacturer's instructions for making gelato.
9. Garnish with fruits. Chocolate, mint or whatever you like. Bon Appetite!

# Banana-Cinnamon Gelato

*Prep Time: 20 minutes*

*Total Time: 5-8 hours*

*Serves: 8*

*Effort: Not much*

**Ingredients:**
- 4 bananas
- 1 and 1/3 cup milk
- 1 and ½ heavy cream
- 4 cinnamon sticks
- ¼ cup maple syrup
- ¼ cup date honey
- dark and white chocolate for garnish

**Directions:**
1. Peel ripe bananas, cut them, pour with maple syrup and bake under a grill for 20-25 minutes.
2. Stir date honey into the baked bananas and beat the mixture with a blender.
3. Add the cinnamon stick to the milk and bring to a boil. Remove from heat, cover and let to steep.
4. Combine banana puree with flavored milk.
5. Chill the cream and beat it properly until thick and frothy. Mix with milk-banana mixture.
6. Pour the mixture into your ice maker and churn according the manufacturer's directions.
7. Garnish with dark and white chocolate when serve. Bon Appetite!

# Delicate Gelato with Pineapple and Coconut Milk

*Prep Time: 40 minutes*

*Total Time: about 5 hours*

*Serves: 4*

*Effort: Not much*

**Ingredients:**
- 1 teaspoon corn starch
- ½ cup sugar
- 4 egg yolks
- 1 cup pineapple chopped finely
- 1 cup heavy cream
- 1 cup coconut milk

**Directions:**
1. Whisk egg yolks with sugar and corn starch.
2. Bring coconut milk to a boil and combine with egg mixture.
3. Heat it on a water bath until thickens.
4. Let your future ice cream cool to the room temperature and place it to a freezer for 15 minutes.
5. Chill the cream and beat it until frothy.
6. Puree the pineapple in a blender, take 2/3 cup of puree and place it to the fridge for 20 minutes.
7. Combine egg mixture with pineapple puree and cream.
8. Stir thoroughly and then transfer the mixture into the ice creamer following the manufacturer's instructions.
9. Serve immediately or keep it in the freezer.

# Blackcurrant Sorbet with Red Wine

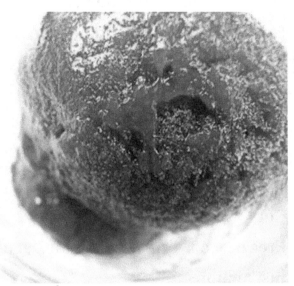

*Prep Time:* 45 minutes

*Total Time: 3-4 hours*

*Serves: 6*

*Effort: Not much*

**Ingredients:**
- 2 cups blackcurrants
- 1 and ½ cup red wine
- ½ cup sugar
- 1 teaspoon lemon juice
- 1 cup water
- 2 cloves
- 2 peppercorns

**Directions:**
1. In a saucepan combine wine, water, sugar, lemon juice, cloves and peppercorns. Bring to a boil and simmer for 25-30 minutes. Remove spices and cool.
2. Pour wine mixture in a blender bowl, add blackcurrants.
3. Beat until smooth and strain to remove seeds.
4. Cool in a fridge and transfer to the ice maker. Freeze according to the manufacturer's instructions.

## Orange-Honey Sorbet

*Prep Time:* 20 minutes

*Total Time:* 3-5 hours

*Serves:* 10

*Effort: Not much*

**Ingredients:**
- 2 oranges
- 1 lemon
- 2-3 tablespoon honey
- 1 tablespoon ginger, peeled and chopped finely
- cayenne pepper to taste

**Directions:**
1. Thoroughly peel oranges, remove all inner skins, chop in small cubes.
2. Do the same with lemon.
3. Place oranges and lemon pulp into a freezer for an hour or two. Once frozen, take it out and let melt for 20 minutes.
4. Place fruits, ginger, honey and a pinch of cayenne pepper into a blender bowl. Process until smooth. Be careful with cayenne pepper, it's very spicy!!
5. We get very delicious ice puree. Enjoy!

# Redcurrant Sorbet

*Prep Time: 10 minutes*

*Total Time: 3-4 hours*

*Serves: 4*

*Effort: Not much*

**Ingredients:**
- 2 tablespoons sugar
- 2 cups redcurrant
- 1 and ½ dessert wine

**Directions:**
1. Whisk redcurrant, dessert wine and sugar in a blender bowl. Beat until smooth.
2. Strain through a sieve to remove seeds.

3. Chill in a fridge and transfer fruit mixture to your ice cream maker. Freeze following the manufacturer's instructions.

## Mango-Peach Sorbet

*Prep Time: 20 minutes*

*Total Time: 3-4 hours*

*Serves: 1 quart*

*Effort: Not much*

**Ingredients:**
- 1 cup sugar
- ½ cup water
- 2 and ½ cup peach, peeled and chopped finely

- 2 and ½ cup mango, peeled and chopped finely
- ¼ cup lime juice

**Directions:**
1. Water with sugar cook in a saucepan over medium-low heat until sugar completely dissolves. Bring to a boil, simmer for 1 minute.
2. Peach and mango process in a food processor until smooth.
3. Transfer the fruit puree to the saucepan with syrup, add lime juice and stir properly.
4. Place the mixture into an ice maker and freeze according the manufacturer's directions.
5. Keep in a freezer.

# Watermelon Sorbet with Mint

***Prep Time:*** **35 minutes**
***Total Time : 3-4 hours***
***Serves: 5***
***Effort: Not much***
**Ingredients:**
- 4 cups watermelon, chopped in cubes, without seeds
- ½ cup sugar
- ¼ cup fresh mint

**Directions:**
1. Combine all ingredients in blender, churn until smooth.
2. Pour the fruit mixture into your ice cream maker, spin according to the manufacturer's instructions.
3. Keep sorbet in a freezer.

# Sparkling Wine Sorbet

***Prep Time: 30 minutes***

***Total Time: about 5 hours***

***Serves: 4***

***Effort: Not much***

**Ingredients:**
- 1 and ½ cup Sparkling wine (Italian Prosecco)
- 1 lemon juice
- 1 lemon zest
- ¾ cup white sugar
- 2/3 cup water
- lemon and lime for garnish

**Directions:**
1. Pour sugar into a saucepan, add water and lemon zest. Set on a low heat, cook, stirring for 2-3 minutes. Remove from heat, strain to get rid of zest, let cool.
2. Add lemon juice and wine to syrup in the saucepan. Stir, pour into an ice cream maker according to the manufacturer's instructions.

## Strawberry Sorbet

*Prep Time:   40 minutes*
*Total Time: about 4-5 hours*
*Serves: 6*
*Effort:  Easy*

**Ingredients:**
- 1/3 cup water
- 1/3 cup sugar
- 2 and ½ cups strawberry
- 1 tablespoon lemon juice
- 1 tablespoon liquor Grand Marnier (if desired)

**Directions:**
1. Combine water and sugar in a small saucepan. Simmer over a medium-low heat until sugar completely dissolves and 1 minute after that.
2. Chill the syrup in a fridge.
3. Puree strawberry in a blender, add lemon juice and liquor. Place into the fridge to chill.
4. Combine strawberry puree with the syrup. Pour the mixture into an ice maker and spin according the manufacturer's instructions.
5. Keep sorbet in a freezer.

# Raspberry Sorbet

*Prep Time: 15 minutes*

*Total Time: 3-4 hours*

*Serves: 4*

*Effort: Not much*

**Ingredients:**
- 1 and ⅓ cup raspberry
- ¾ cup sugar
- ½ lemon
- 1 cup water

**Directions:**
1. Combine water with sugar in a saucepan. Bring to a boil and simmer for 7 minutes. Don't stir.

2. Pour the syrup into a bowl and let chill for 30-50 minutes.
3. Add raspberry to the syrup. Puree with a blender.
4. Strain through a sieve to get rid of seeds.
5. Squeeze juice out of one lemon into the mixture and stir.
6. Pour into the airtight container and place into a freezer.
7. Churn every 15-20 minutes for 3-4 hours if you don't have an ice cream maker.

## Melon Sorbet

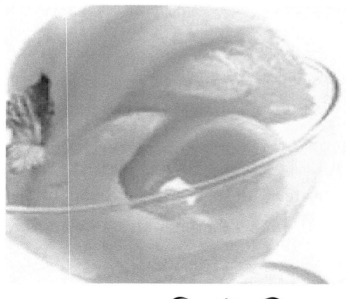

*Prep Time:* 20 minutes

*Total Time: about 4 hours*

*Serves: 6*

*Effort: Not much*

**Ingredients:**
- 3 and ½ cups melon, peeled and chopped finely.
- 5 tablespoons lemon juice
- 6 tablespoons sugar
- 6-8 tablespoons water

**Directions:**
1. Cook a syrup with water and sugar. Chill.
2. Puree melon pulp in blender, add lemon juice and chilled syrup. Churn thoroughly.
3. Freeze in an ice cream maker according to the manufacturer's instructions.

# Blueberry Sorbet

*Prep Time: 20 minutes*

*Total Time: 3 hours*

*Serves: 4*

*Effort: Not much*

**Ingredients:**
- 3 cups blueberry
- ½ cup sugar
- ½ cup water
- 1 tablespoon lemon juice

**Directions:**
1. Combine water and sugar in a small saucepan. Simmer over a medium-low heat until sugar

completely dissolves. Cook for 5 1 minute after that. Remove from heat. Chill.
2. Puree blueberry in a blender. Combine with sugar syrup and lemon juice.
3. Pour the mixture into the bowl of an ice cream maker and spin according to the manufacturer's instructions.
4. Keep sorbet in a freezer.
5. Garnish before serving.

## Granite Carcade

*Prep Time: 35 minutes*
*Total Time : 3-4 hours*
*Serves: 4*

*Effort: Not much*

**Ingredients:**
- 4 Carcade tea bags
- ½ cup Cranberry syrup
- ¼ cup cane sugar
- 2 oranges
- fresh mint for serving

**Directions:**
1. Brew dense and steeped tea, pouring 1 and 1/3 cups of boiling water over 4 teabags of red tea Carcade.
2. Add sugar, orange zest and juice. Let steep.
3. Strain the tea.
4. Combine the strained tea with Cranberry syrup.
5. Pour the mixture into a wide container so that its depth does not exceed 2-3 cm and place it into a freezer.
6. In 20 minutes stir the mixture with a fork.
7. Do it every 30-40 minutes until granita is completely frozen but at the same time fluffy as snow.
8. Serve in cocktail glasses. Garnish with mint, chocolate or whatever you like.

# Granite with Lime and Orange

**Prep Time:** 25 minutes

**Total Time:** 3-4 hours

**Serves: 4**

**Effort: Not much**

**Ingredients:**
- 2 cups water
- ½ cup lime juice
- ½ cup orange juice
- ½ cup sugar
- 2 tablespoons honey
- melissa, mint, lavender, cherry leaves if desired

**Directions:**
1. Cook a syrup. Combine 1 cup water with sugar, bring to a boil, add cherry leaves, melissa, mint, lavender. In 5 minutes add the remaining water, bring to a boil, add lime and orange juice.
2. Strain, chill, add honey if desired. Place into a freezer for 3-4 hours.
3. In the process of freezing one time take granite out of the freezer, break the ice with a fork or a blender. Grind ready granite to the state of fragrant snow and serve immediately.

## Peach Granita

*Prep Time:* 10 minutes

*Total Time :* 3 hours and 10 minutes

*Serves:* 4

*Effort: Not much*

**Ingredients:**
- 4 big peaches
- ½ cup water
- ¼ cup sugar
- 1 tablespoon lemon juice
- a pinch of salt

**Directions:**
1. Peel the peaches, remove pits, and chop the pulp into large chunks.
2. Combine the peaches with water, lemon juice and a pinch of salt in a blender and puree the mixture until smooth.
3. Pour the mixture into an airtight container and leave in a freezer for 3 hours.
4. Stir the mixture every hour to give your granite the form of friable snow.
5. Garnish before serving.

# Coffee Granite

*Prep Time: 20 minutes*

*Total Time: 5 hours*

*Serves: 2-3*

*Effort: Not much*

**Ingredients:**
- 1 cup of good strong coffee
- ¼ cup cane sugar
- whipped cream for garnish

**Directions:**
1. Make a cup of really strong coffee. Add sugar, stir until completely dissolved. Let it cool.
2. Pour the chilled coffee into a container good for freezing and transfer it to a freezer.

3. In 30 minutes take the container out. There will be an ice crust on the coffee surface. Crush this crust with a knife and return the container back to the freezer.
4. Repeat this procedure every hour 4-5 times. As a result, you'll have a lot of icy crumbs and that is exactly what we need.
5. These crumbs- coffee granite can be served both in pure form and with whipped cream in serving glasses. Have a nice rest!

## Pomegranate Granita

*Prep Time: 25 minutes*
*Total Time : 3 hours*

*Serves: 6*

*Effort: Not much*

**Ingredients:**
- 2 cups fresh pomegranate juice
- 1 tablespoon fresh lemon juice
- ¼ cup agave nectar
- ¼ cup pomegranate seeds for garnish

**Directions:**
1. Whisk all the juice and agave nectar and pour the mixture into a metal cake shape with a diameter of 20 cm or another container of the same size. Put for an hour in the freezer.
2. Remove from the freezer and stir the frozen mixture with a fork.
3. Then put it in the freezer again.
4. Repeat the procedure every 15 minutes for two hours.
5. In the end, you should get a solid mixture, similar to sorbet flakes.
6. You can put granite into freeze overnight, and then crumble before serving.
7. Serve, spread out in six glasses or cups and garnish with pomegranate seeds.

8. Enjoy your pomegranate granite. No sugar! No milk! Only health benefits ☺

## Apple Granita

***Prep Time: 1 hour***

***Total Time: 3-4 hours***

***Serves: 6***

***Effort: Not much***

**Ingredients:**
- 1.4 lbs apple
- 2 and ½ cups water
- ¾ cup sugar
- 1 lemon

**Directions:**
1. Put sugar and a little bit of lemon zest (grate the lemon on a large grater) in a small pot of water. Heat and stir until the sugar dissolves.
2. Let cool.
3. Strain to remove the lemon zest.
4. Peel and core the apples, place into the pan and cook for 5 minutes until soft. Let cool in a bowl.
5. Puree the chilled apples with syrup in a blender, add 1 lemon juice.
6. Freeze for 1 hour.
7. Remove from the freezer and stir with a fork to crush the crystals.
8. Return to the freezer for another hour, then mix again.
9. Repeat 3-4 times until the correct texture is obtained, then freeze until needed.

# Granita with Spicy Wine

*Prep Time:  30 minutes*

*Total Time: 3-4 hours*

*Serves: 6*

*Effort: Not much*

**Ingredients:**
- 3 cups dry red wine
- 1/2 cup  sugar
- 1 stick cinnamon
- 2 cloves
- ½ teaspoon allspice
- ½ teaspoon black peppercorns

**Directions:**

1. In a saucepan combine wine, sugar, a stick cinnamon, clove, allspice and black pepper.
2. Put the pan on medium heat and cook, stirring, until the sugar dissolves.
3. Cook 5 minutes more, then remove from heat and allow to steep for 15 minutes.
4. Strain the mixture into a square baking dish and completely freeze for about 5 hours.
5. Scrape the granite with a fork and spread it into glasses. Enjoy!

## White Grape Granita

*Prep Time: 40 minutes*
*Total Time: 5 hours*

*Serves: 8*

*Effort: Some*

**Ingredients:**
- 2 lbs grape without seeds
- 1 cup Champagne or any other white sparkling wine
- 2 tablespoons lemon juice
- 3 tablespoons sugar

**Directions:**
1. Puree grape in your food processor until smooth.
2. Strain it through a metal sieve to get rid of skins.
3. Combine fruit mixture with wine, lemon juice and sugar, stir properly and pour into glass container.
4. Place container into a freezer for 3 hours.
5. Stir the frozen mixture with a fork and serve immediately.

# Watermelon Granita

*Prep Time:* 15 minutes

*Total Time:* 4-5 hours

*Serves:* 6

*Effort: Some*

**Ingredients:**
- 8 lbs watermelon
- 1/2 cup rum
- 4 limes
- 1 cup sugar
- ¾ cup water

**Directions:**
1. Cook a syrup in a saucepan.

Bring water with sugar to a boil and simmer until sugar completely dissolves.
2. Squeeze juice out of limes, pour it into the syrup, stir and let chill.
3. Peel and pit the watermelon.
4. Puree the watermelon pulp in a blender until smooth. Stir in rum and churn again.
5. Combine watermelon puree with chilled syrup, stir and pour into a wide and low container and place into a freezer.
6. Before serving beat the frozen granite in the blender once more.

## Grapefruit Granita

**Prep Time:** 15 minutes

**Total Time:** 5 hours

**Serves:** 3

**Effort:** Some

**Ingredients:**
- 2 grapefruits
- 2/3 cup water
- 2-5 tablespoons sugar

**Directions:**
1. Squeeze juice out of grapefruits. Strain it through a fine sieve to get rid of inner skins.
2. Cook a syrup with water and sugar ( sugar to your taste) , chill it.
3. Combine the syrup with the juice and pour the mixture into a low container for freezing. Cover and place to a freezer.
4. In an hour or so stir the mixture with a fork and leave in a freezer again.
5. Repeat this every hour so that the granite gets an even crystalline texture.

## Your Gift!

We want to show our appreciation that you support our work, so we have put together a gift for you.

http://bit.ly/2tHoyEJ

Just visit the link above to download it now.

We know you will love this gift.
Thanks!

www.ingramcontent.com/pod-product-compliance
Lightning Source LLC
LaVergne TN
LVHW011200070225
803202LV00011B/910